101

GHOST JOKES

Lisa Eisenberg & Katy Hall

Illustrated by Don Orehek

SCHOLASTIC INC.
New York Toronto London Auckland Sydney

To our little ghouls,
Annie, Kate, and Leigh

Cover illustration by Robert DeMichiell.

ISBN 0-590-99827-7

Text copyright © 1988 by Katy Hall and Lisa Eisenberg.
Illustrations copyright © 1996 by Scholastic Inc.

12 11 10 9 8 7 6 5 4 3 2 1   10   6 7 8 9/9 0 1/0

Printed in the U.S.A.   01

101
GHOST JOKES

LIFE IN GHOST TOWN

What ghost helped the Little Leaguers win their game?

The team spirit!

What day of the week do ghosts look forward to?

Moanday!

Who greets you at the door of a
haunted house?

A ghost host!

What did the ghost bride throw to her bridesmaids?

Her boo-quet!

What did the guard at the haunted house say?

"Halt! Who ghost there?"

Ed: What do you call it when a ghost makes an error?

Ted: A grave mistake?

Ed: No — a boo-boo!

Why did the ghosts put a fence around the cemetery?

People were dying to get in!

Why don't ghosts go out in the rain?

It dampens their spirits!

Who represents ghosts in Congress?

The Spooker of the House!

What spirit serves food on a plane?

An airline ghostess!

What did the mother ghost tell her little ghosts?

Don't spook until you are spooken to!

What did the mother ghost say when the little ghosts got into the car?

"Boo-kle up your sheet-belts!"

What does a little ghost call his mother and father?

His trans-parents!

What do little ghosts like to play with instead of Frisbees?

Boo-merangs!

FAVORITE HAUNTS

What kind of ghost haunts
skyscrapers?

High spirits!

Where do fashionable ghosts shop for
sheets?

At boo-tiques!

What rides do little spirits like best
at the amusement park?

The roller ghoster!

11

What would you get if you crossed a cocker spaniel, a French poodle, and a ghost?

A cocker-poodle-boo!

What would you get if you crossed a chicken and a ghost?

A peck-a-boo!

What would you get if you crossed a ghost and an owl?

Something that frightens people — but doesn't give a hoot!

13

Why wasn't the ghost successful?

He didn't believe in himself!

Why wasn't the ghost popular at parties?

He wasn't much to look at!

Where do ghosts go on vacation in August?

To the sea ghost!

Who writes all the books about haunted houses?

Ghostwriters, who else?

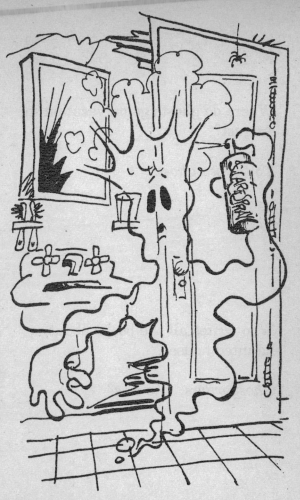

How do well-groomed ghosts keep
their hair in place?

With scare spray!

GHOST TO GHOST

What did one ghost say to the other ghost?

Do you really believe in people?

What country is haunted by ghosts?

No country — just a terror-tory!

Who protects the shores where spirits live?

The Ghost Guard!

18

What patriotic song do ghosts like best?

"America the Boo-tiful!"

What fairy tale do all ghosts like best?

Sleeping Boo-ty!

What happens on Broadway when a ghost haunts a theater?

The actors get stage fright!

Ghost 1: My girlfriend is a medium.
Ghost 2: That so? Well, mine's a
large!

What do ghost cheerleaders say?

Rah! Rah! Sis-boo-*bah!*

What kind of music do ghosts write?

Sheet music!

What would you call the expression
on the face of a poker-playing ghost?

Deadpan!

GHOSTLY
KNOCK-EM-DEADS!

Knock, knock!
Who's there?
Soup!
Soup who?
Soup-er natural beings are in this
   house!

Knock, knock!
Who's there?
Dawn.
Dawn who?
Dawn leave me alone!

Knock, knock!
Who's there?
Owl.
Owl who?
Owl you know to let me in if I don't
   knock?

Knock, knock!
Who's there?
Dismay.
Dismay who?
Dismay seem funny to you, but *I'm*
   scared!

Luke out! There's one right behind you!

Knock, knock!
Who's there?
Police!
Police who?
Police let me in there!

Knock, knock!
Who's there?
Max!
Max who?
Max no difference who I am! Just let
 me in!

Who's there?

Ken.

Ken who?

Ken I hide in the closet with you?

Knock, knock!
Who's there?
Radio.
Radio who?
Radio not, here I come!

THE SPIRIT
OF THE PAST

Spirit: May I haunt your castle?
Queen: Certainly — be my ghost!

King: How far can a ghost walk into a cemetery?
Queen: Just halfway.... Then he's walking out of the cemetery!

Queen: It's so hot in the castle tonight. Won't you please tell me a ghost story?

King: A ghost story? But why?

Queen: Oh, you know! Ghost stories are always so chilling!

King: Oooooohhh! I've just seen a three-hundred-pound ghost!

Queen: Gads! What does a three-hundred-pound ghost look like?

King: Like nothing I've ever seen!

Queen: What goes 'oob'?
King: I don't know. What?
Queen: A ghost in reverse!

Queen: What do you say to a
two-headed ghost?
King: Boo! Boo!

U.S. GHOST OFFICE

Where should you send a ghost's mail?

To the dead-letter department!

What street does a ghost live on?

A dead-end street!

In what language should you write to a ghost?

In Latin — it's a dead language!

How should you begin the letter?

"Tomb it may concern!"

What kind of letters do ghosts like to send?

Chain letters!

Why wouldn't the mailman deliver
the ghost's letter?

He was on his coffin break!

How do ghosts like to send their
letters?

Scare mail — or parcel ghost!

GREAT PLACES
TO HAUNT

Massacre-chusetts

Don't miss Booston!

Gory-gone

Right on the West Ghost!
And don't skip the Petrified Forest!

New Hexico

Plan to stay a spell!

MORE PLACES
TO HAUNT

Moantana

Truly terrifying scenery!

Wy-ooohhh-ming

Lots of moantains to climb!

New Hauntshire

Be sure to visit Discord, the capital
  city!

SICK OF GHOSTS!

Nurse: Doctor, there's a ghost in
your waiting room!
Doctor: Tell him I can't see him!

Why was the little ghost crying in the
doctor's office?

*She didn't want to get her boo-ster
shot!*

Why did the doctor tell the sad ghosts
to take lots of rides in an elevator?

He thought it would raise their spirits!

Why did the doctor tell the ghost to
go on a diet?

So she could keep her ghoulish figure!

Ghost: Doctor, I feel faint!
Doctor: Well, I guess you do. You're
  white as a sheet!

What kind of doctor does a ghost go to?

A witch doctor!

Why did the ghost go to the foot doctor?

He had an in-groan toenail!

Did the doctor know the ghost was sick?

Yes, he was dead certain!

Ghost: Doctor, why am I so lonely?
Doctor: Because you've got no body!

GHOST CHILL-DREN

How do ghost babies cry?

BOO-hoo! BOO-hoo!

What song do ghost children like best?

"A Haunting We Will Go!"

What kind of horses do ghost kids like to ride?

Night-mares!

What do ghost babies wear on their feet?

BOO-tees!

What did they call the two little twin ghosts that rang all the doorbells on Halloween?

Dead ringers!

MORE GHOSTLY KNOCK-EM-DEADS

Knock, knock.
Who's there?
Sarah!
Sarah who?
Sarah ghost in the house?

Knock, knock.
Who's there?
Beef.
Beef who?
Beef-ore I tell you, let me come in!

Who's there?

Orange.

Orange who?

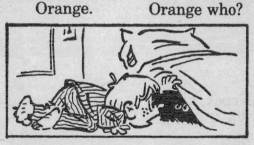

Orange you going to let me hide
under the bed with you?

Knock, knock!
Who's there?
Celeste!
Celeste who?
Celeste time I'll warn you before I
   come in!

Knock, knock!
Who's there?
Heaven.
Heaven who?
Heaven you heard enough of these
   silly knock-knock jokes?

THE UNFRIENDLY RESTAURHAUNT AND COFFIN SHOP
MOAN-U

A die-ning delight that will lift your
  spirits!

SAND-WITCHES

Boo-loney
Boo-gels and Scream Cheese
Hallow-weenies
Liver-worst

BOO-VERAGES

Milk Shaaaakes
Ice Scream Floats
Orange Crrrush

HEX-TRAS

Clammy on the Half Shell
Chilllled Tomb-ato Juice
*Devil*ed Eggs

SOUPS AND SALADS

L-eeek! Soup
Cream of Asparaghost
Arti-Choke Hearts
Lettuce Alone Salad
Marinated Brussel Shouts

SIGHED DISHES

Baked Beings
Cre-mated Spinach

DESS-HURTS

Creep Suzettes
Banana Scream Pie
Sheet Cake
Key Slime Pie
Hot Sludge Shun-dae

TODAY'S SPE-CHILLS

Spook-ghetti
Southern Fright Chicken
Ghoul-lash
Turkey with *Grave*-y
Pasta-way

Cus-tomb-ers: We accept Die-ners
Club, Monster Card, and American
Hex-press Credit Cards

UNFRIENDLY'S BREAKFAST MOAN-U

Breakfast Served
from Midnight to 3 A.M. Daily

CEREALS

Ghost Toasties with Evaporated Milk
Shrouded Wheat
Scream of Wheat

EGGS

Terri-fried Eggs — Over Easy
Scream-bled Eggs
Three-moan-it Soft-booled Eggs
Stormy-side-up Eggs
Eggs Boonidict

A HOST OF GHOSTS

What is one room a ghost's house
doesn't need?

A living room!

What did they say about the ghost's
house party?

It was a howling success!

What happens when a banana sees a
ghost?

The banana splits!

What kind of friends did the ghost
invite to his party?

Oh, just anyone he could dig up!

How do ghosts stay in shape?

By daily exorcism!

Imagine you were trapped in a spooky haunted house full of ghosts. What would you do?

Stop imagining!

What do you get from a two-headed ghost?

Double talk!

Why is the letter G scary?

It turns a host into a ghost!

What became of the girl who drank
shellac and died?

*She became a ghost with a lovely
finish!*

What kind of raincoat does a ghost
wear on a dark and stormy night?

A wet one!

Why wouldn't the ghost lady get a permanent wave for her hair?

*She wanted her curls to be super-*natural!

What time is it when the clock strikes 13?

Midnight, Pacific Ghost Time!

What would you do if you were walking down the street and saw three ghosts following you?

Hope it was Halloween!

What do ghosts do to amuse themselves?

They tell "people stories"!

What should an elegant ghost do if she can't afford mink?

Wear wolf! (werewolf)

Why aren't many ghosts arrested?

It's hard to pin anything on them!

What do you call a dozen ghosts?

A bunch of boo-boos!

BEST CHILLERS!

Books To Die for . . .

Little Boo Peep
Dr. Spook's Advice
Moldy Lox and the Three Bears
Winnie the Boo
The Weirdzard of Oz
Ra-moana Forever
Little Wo-moan
Pin-ooohh!-chio
Dr. Boolittle
Tails of Peter Rabid
Black Booty

A GHOST'S
TV SCHEDULE

 7 A.M.: Good Moan-ing America!
          on A-Boo-C
 8 A.M.: Ghoul-igans Island
 9 A.M.: Father Knows Beast
10 A.M.: Name That Tomb
11 A.M.: Squeal of Fortune
12 P.M.: Noose at Noon
 1 P.M.: The Newly-dead Game

2 P.M.: The Broody Bunch
3 P.M.: Bury Manilow Spe-chill
6 P.M.: Entertainment Tomb-night
7 P.M.: Groaning Pains
8 P.M.: Dead of the Class
9 P.M.: Boonanza
10 P.M.: St. Else-scare
12 A.M.: Late Night
with David Lettermoan

SC-GOUL DAYS

Why did the ghost ask the teacher if he could change his seat?

He wanted to sit next to his ghoul-friend!

Why did the ghost student collapse in class?

He was so tired, he was dead on his feet!

What kind of trees do ghost students study?

Ceme-trees!

Ghost Teacher: If a ghostbuster came after you, what steps would you take?
Ghost Student: BIG steps!

How did the ghost teacher explain the lesson on walking through walls?

She went through it again and again!

What song do little ghosts sing in kindergarten?

"Boo Boo Black Sheep!"

What game do baby ghosts play in nursery school?

Peek-a-BOO!

Why did the little ghost flunk his
math test?

He used invisible ink!

Why didn't the teacher believe the
little ghost's excuses?

She could see right through him!

Why did the little ghost flunk his spelling test?

He made too many boo-boos!

What do ghosts like to study in high school?

Boo-ology!

Why did the students study the ghost for half an hour every day?

Because he was history!

GHOSTLY GIGGLES

What do you get if you cross an angry ghost with a vampire?

Nothing. You should never cross an angry ghost!

What do you get if you cross a ghost with a cheetah?

A sheetah!

What do you get if you cross a ghost with a refrigerator?

A sheet of ice!

What shows do ghosts like best?

Phantom-mimes!

What did the ghost say to his girlfriend?

Baby, you're outa sight!

What do the ghosts of dead
gingerbread men wear?

Cookie sheets!

What happened to the ghost who
swallowed a frog?

*Nothing. The ghost had already
croaked!*

Where do you find a missing ghost?

At his favorite haunt!

What does a ghost take when he has the flu?

Coffin drops!

Why did the little girl ghost haunt baseball fields?

Because diamonds are a ghoul's best friend!

Where do ghosts like to swim?

In the Dead Sea!

What happened when the girl ghost
met the boy ghost?

It was love at first fright!

How do ghosts go through locked
doors?

With skeleton keys!

93

Why was the ghost a coward?

She didn't have any guts!

Why did the ghost go to the astrologer?

She wanted to know her horrorscope!